Contents

Cover: M. H. Baillie Scott, *House for an Art Lover* competition entry.
A copy of this rare 1902 folio of designs was acquired by the Trust in 2008.
© Lakeland Arts Trust 2009.

Above: The Main Hall, showing some of the similarities to
Baillie Scott's entry for *House for an Art Lover*.
© Lakeland Arts Trust 2009.

The Re-awakening

Blackwell (1898 – 1900) was purchased by an independent charity, the Lakeland Arts Trust, in February 1999 so that it could be rescued from oblivion, restored and opened for the public to enjoy. Altogether, the project took four and a half years and cost almost £3,500,000. It is the only building by the architect Mackay Hugh Baillie Scott (1865-1945) that is open to the public, and it is one of his largest and most important surviving works in this country. Since it opened on the 4th July 2001 Blackwell has won two prestigious architecture awards, from the Royal Institute of British Architects and from The Civic Trust. In 2005 it also won the Northwest Small Visitor Attraction of the Year award.

Baillie Scott was an important figure in the development of European domestic architecture, designing Arts & Crafts buildings, furniture and furnishings. The Arts and Crafts Movement, a reaction against the increasing dominance of mechanisation brought about by the Industrial Revolution, was championed by John Ruskin (1819-1900) and William Morris (1834-1896), the 'fathers' of the movement, who sought to re-establish the importance and worth of designer-craftsmen. They advocated a simpler life, in which the domestic sphere would be a place of harmony and beauty. In line with this ethos, Arts & Crafts architecture was distinguishable from mainstream architecture by hallmarks such as the use of local materials, reference to regional building methods and the employment of local craftsmen.

Blackwell was designed at a key moment, as architects in Britain and Europe began to look afresh at how houses functioned and the way people lived in the home. The twentieth century saw many rapid changes in domestic arrangements, most significantly in the move away from employing servants, changes in the family as a unit, and the development of modern conveniences such as en-suite bathrooms and electrical appliances. Most houses have been altered to accommodate these changes - and the wealthy owners of large houses are usually the first to update with the latest trends. It is therefore all the more remarkable, and rare for a house of this period, that Blackwell has largely escaped any alterations and almost all of its original decorative features have survived.

Above: Carved oak ceiling boss in the Main Hall
Opposite: Blackwell in 1995 before restoration © Charlotte Wood 1995

"In the house the fire is a substitute for the sun... The cheerfulness we experience from the fire is akin to the delight sunlight brings."

M. H. Baillie Scott, *Houses and Gardens*, 1906

Above: William de Morgan, *Anemone* tile, c.1890s,
Oliver Thompson Gallery
Below: Stained glass, Dining Room
Opposite: Inglenook fireplace with original *Anemone* tiles by
William de Morgan, Oliver Thompson Gallery

Blackwell is regarded as a pivotal building in the oeuvre of
Baillie Scott and was the largest commission of the early phase of
his career. Built as a grand holiday home, it represented a major
opportunity to realise many of his ideas which, up until then, he had
only produced in watercolours, drawings or imaginary schemes.

What makes Blackwell particularly special is that it was designed as
a holiday home rather than a main residence. The design, therefore,
was not restricted by many of the domestic necessities most
large houses required. This commission from a wealthy patron,
unfettered by tiresome practicalities, really did give Baillie Scott the
opportunity to show what he could do, and all of this in the beautiful
setting among the Lakeland fells.

As soon as the Lakeland Arts Trust acquired Blackwell, research
was started to investigate how it would have looked originally.
Various photographs of Blackwell are included in Baillie Scott's
book, *Houses and Gardens*, published in 1906, although there is
very little other photographic evidence. Paint scrapes were taken
and analysed to discover the original decorative schemes, and a
great deal of other detective work was undertaken by a team of
specialist experts. Many of the original features, such as the
William de Morgan tiled fireplaces, had simply been boarded up,
and most of the beautiful oak floors were laid over with utilitarian
carpet tiles. There were original examples of practically every
decorative and functional element, and where some were missing,
such as the brass leaf-shaped door handles, replicas were made by
a local blacksmith.

The Trust did not inherit any of the original furniture with the house;
however, from the early photographs we can see that the Holts
did not follow whole-heartedly their architect's ideals in respect
of furnishing. Much of what they had appears to be Regency
or Victorian, and mostly it was mahogany rather than oak, the
preferred timber of the Arts & Crafts designers. Luckily, quite a
number of Baillie Scott's watercolours of interiors he designed have
been published in colour. And it is these that have been used to
inform the way in which the period rooms have been furnished. It
was a much more deliberate, and rather lean, arrangement that
Blackwell's architect favoured and, following these principles, the
Trust has brought important pieces of Arts & Crafts furniture and
objects into the house.

A Grand Holiday Home

Blackwell was built as a rural holiday retreat for the Manchester brewery owner, Sir Edward Holt (1849 - 1928), his wife Elizabeth and their five children. A wealthy industrialist, Holt was active in local government and had the honour of being made Lord Mayor of Manchester for two consecutive years, 1907-9. Sir Edward, who was made a baronet in 1916, worked for numerous good causes, helping to improve buildings, libraries, water and sewage works.

Holt's most memorable charity work was in the foundation of the Manchester and District Radium Institute, later known as the Holt Radium Institute and Christie's Hospital. Other charitable gestures included providing holidays at Blackwell for underprivileged orphans from the Jubilee School for Girls, who had little experience of the countryside, having been brought up in Manchester's slums.

Before the arrival of the railway at Windermere in 1847, Bowness was only a small village. The advent of the railway brought with it growing numbers of tourists, who were lured to the Lake District by the romantic scenery, boating on the lakes, and associations with Wordsworth and Ruskin. Many northern industrialists also sought second homes here. The end of the nineteenth century thus saw a huge boom in large-scale house building in the Lake District, particularly along the eastern shores of Windermere.

It would appear that the house was commissioned not just for its beautiful setting, but also because of its location. Sir Edward Holt worked with the Manchester Waterworks Committee on the development of the reservoir at Thirlmere, near Keswick, which was completed in 1894. This subsequently led him to recommend the acquisition of the Haweswater Estate, and another large reservoir was eventually created. These developments were to revolutionise the supply of fresh water to the suburbs of Manchester. Blackwell provided Holt with the perfect Lake District base from which to monitor their progress. He also took an active interest in the local community and became a JP for Windermere in 1907.

Little is known about the craftsmen who worked on the construction of Blackwell as most of Baillie Scotts records were destroyed by fire later in his career.

Above: Sir Edward Holt as Lord Mayor of Manchester in 1907
Opposite: The wrought iron Main Gate with Edward Holt's monogram.
© Nick Wood 2005

"… Blackwell is a building of international significance as well as the masterpiece of rare imagination and subtlety."

Gavin Stamp, *Crafts*, July 2001

Above: Lady Elizabeth Holt
Below: The White Drawing Room at the beginning of the 20th century
Opposite: The Main Hall at the beginning of the 20th century showing the original chandelier, designed by Baillie Scott, its whereabouts now unknown

Sir Edward Holt commissioned Simpsons of Kendal to work on the carving and panelling in the interiors at Blackwell, having first visited Arthur W. Simpson in 1894. Arthur Simpson and his son, Hubert, ran 'The Handicrafts', creating fine Arts & Crafts wood carvings and furniture, much of which can still be found in Lake District and Lancashire churches and homes. Their workshop flourished from 1895 until 1952 when it finally closed. They were also commissioned to produce carvings for St Margaret's Church in Prestwich, the town of the Holt family's main residence.

Blackwell's interiors were not furnished as Baillie Scott would have intended, but with Regency and Victorian pieces already belonging to the Holt family. A rare early photograph of the Main Hall shows it furnished complete with hunting trophies! When the Holts moved out their furniture went too, so today Blackwell is furnished with objects that the architect might have chosen, based on his published watercolours of house interiors. Baillie Scott admired old houses and antique furniture, and a careful study of these helped inform his architectural style. He also often incorporated elements from earlier periods into his designs for houses, such as the eighteenth century fire grate in the Dining Room or the panelling in the Main Hall that was reclaimed from St Mary's Church. At Blackwell we have thus followed the architect's principles, placing Arts & Crafts furniture of the period alongside seventeenth century oak pieces from the Abbot Hall Art Gallery collection.

The Holts visited Blackwell regularly in the first years of the twentieth century. Joseph Holt, the eldest son, was a keen oarsman and also enjoyed racing a 22-foot yacht, the Ibis, which is listed in the Windermere Yacht Club records of 1904. The house design included a boathouse on the lake (now privately owned) where they kept a steam launch, which is very similar to S. L. Osprey, currently being restored by the Lakeland Arts Trust as part of the Windermere Steamboat Salvage Scheme. The Holt's happy period of leisured living was to be cut short when the eldest son and heir, Joseph, was killed during the First World War. After this the family visited Blackwell less and less frequently. The death of Sir Edward Holt in 1928 saw Blackwell inherited by his second son, also Edward, who decided to lease it out.

The Architect -
M. H. Baillie Scott

Above: Mackay Hugh Baillie Scott (1865 - 1945). Photograph c.1906
Opposite: Doorway leading from the Main Hall into the Dining Room
© Lakeland Arts Trust / Charlotte Wood 2005

Mackay Hugh Baillie Scott was born at Beards Hill, St Peter's, near Ramsgate, Kent on the 23rd October 1865. He was the eldest of 14 children. His father, also Mackay Hugh Baillie Scott, was a wealthy farmer who owned a large estate in Scotland, as well as a valuable sheep ranch in Australia.

Baillie Scott's architectural career was to span from the 1890s well into the twentieth century. He rose to prominence during the transitional period between the Victorian and Edwardian eras, at a time when society and industry were rapidly changing. He was one of a number of Arts & Crafts artists and architects who looked to the past for a new approach to design, inspired by medieval master builders and craftsmen, and united in the endeavour to improve the quality of people's everyday lives.

Having trained at agricultural college in Cirencester, Baillie Scott was originally destined to take over the management of his father's sheep farm in Australia. However, in 1886 he chose to study architecture instead. From an early age he had shown an interest in nature and the arts, and he spent much of his time sketching the landscape where he grew up, particularly the old country farmhouses and churches. This love of nature and art was to become the foundation of his design philosophy and may partly explain why he chose architecture over agriculture as a career.

In 1886 Baillie Scott was articled to Major Charles E. Davis, the City Architect of Bath. It was perhaps not the best practice in which to serve his apprenticeship, as Davis's architecture was in the High Victorian style and offered few opportunities or indeed challenges, for the young and ambitious Baillie Scott.

The city of Bath, however, did provide some inspiration in its many Roman excavations. The marble tiled floors, which can be seen in the entrance porch and in the fireplace in the White Drawing Room at Blackwell, are reminiscent of Roman mosaics, although it is more likely that they were inspired by the Italian Cosmati floors of the eleventh and twelfth centuries.

"A house may possess that inscrutable quality of the True Romance. Not shallow, showy and pretentious, as most modern mansions are, but full of still, quiet earnestness which seems to lull and soothe the spirit with promises of peace."

M. H. Baillie Scott, 1906

In 1889 Baillie Scott moved to the Isle of Man after the honeymoon trip he made there with his wife Florence. Initially he worked for the surveyor, Fred Sanderson, in Douglas. Being somewhat removed from mainland influences, he was able to develop his own architectural style, as can be seen by the houses he built there, having set up his practice in 1892. These include his own Red House, which showed considerable innovation in planning. He also designed the Majestic Hotel, which was demolished in 2000, and the Castletown Police House.

Baillie Scott's first buildings were, to some extent, influenced by the great Arts & Crafts architects and designers of the day, principally Charles Francis Annesley Voysey (1857-1941), who designed Moor Crag and Broad Leys by the shores of Windermere, not far from Blackwell. He would have seen Voysey's work in magazines such as *The Studio*, to which both men regularly contributed articles on architecture, and in which Baillie Scott's first article appeared in 1895.

His articles in *The Studio* magazine brought Baillie Scott to the attention of a European clientele, and in 1897 he was commissioned to create interior decorations and furnishings for the Grand Duke of Hesse's Palace at Darmstadt. This won the architect an international reputation and several more important commissions abroad. Baillie Scott was also engaged in the design of tapestries and furnishings for the Deutsche Werkstatten in Munich between 1900 and 1914.

Importantly, his first commission after Darmstadt came from Edward Holt, for Blackwell. Drawings of a design for Blackwell were exhibited at the Royal Academy Summer Exhibition of 1898; however, it is possible they were made before he had visited the steep fellside site, as they were drawn on the flat, and without the familiar cylindrical Lakeland chimney pots that we can see at Blackwell today.

When Baillie Scott began work on Blackwell, the Scottish architect, Charles Rennie Mackintosh, who was three years his junior, was also beginning to get commissions. The Hill House at Helensburgh and several other of Mackintosh's designs show similarities with those of Baillie Scott. Both architects entered a German competition to design a Haus eines Kunstfreundes (House for an Art Lover) in 1901. No first prize was awarded, but Baillie Scott

Above: Drawing of Blackwell made for Edward Holt, published in *The Studio*, 1901
Opposite: Blackwell from the original driveway
© Lakeland Arts Trust / Charlotte Wood 2005

won second prize and Mackintosh, who had not complied with all the rules, was given a special prize. It is evident, when looking at his watercolours, that much of the inspiration for the interiors Baillie Scott submitted for the *Haus eines Kunstfreundes* competition came from Blackwell.

Baillie Scott was destined to make a major contribution to the already established Arts & Crafts Movement, and by the time he started work on Blackwell the Arts & Crafts Movement was flourishing in the Lake District. John Ruskin, who had his home at Brantwood by Coniston Water, had done much to support the establishment of the Keswick School of Industrial Art in 1884 as well as the production of Langdale Linen and Ruskin Lace. Another outlet for the Arts & Crafts was Annie Garnett's Spinnery at Bowness. Mrs Holt visited the Spinnery in 1900 and her name appears in the visitors' book, though there appears to have been no record kept of what she might have bought.

As well as designing furniture as part of architectural commissions, Baillie Scott also developed a range of furniture that was made to his designs by the firm of J. P. White in Bedford. His furniture was retailed directly by J. P. White, and also through outlets such as Wylie and Lochhead and Liberty's. Baillie Scott's decision to move from the Isle of Man to Bedford in 1901 may well have been taken in order to supervise work on his range of furniture. The J. P. White *Pyghtle Works* catalogue of that year shows Baillie Scott furniture of striking originality and simplicity. It is not known how much furniture was sold, but the designs had a marked impact upon European and American furniture.

Baillie Scott is perhaps best known in Britain for his later cottage houses. He wanted to provide suitable alternative accommodation for his preferred clientèle, whom he described as *"... people with artistic aspirations but modest incomes..."* and, with this in mind, he opened up the room plan around a spacious living area. He continued to design more modest houses, mostly for the garden suburbs of southern England, until 1939 when, following the death of his wife, he closed his architectural practice.

In addition to Blackwell, Baillie Scott's long list of work includes fourteen houses in Cambridge, twelve houses on the Isle of Man, hotels and farms. Sadly, very few of his original architectural drawings or watercolours survive, as most were lost in two disastrous fires, one resulting from the bombing of his studio in World War II.

Above: Carved oak panelling of rowan berry design (detail), by Simpsons of Kendal, Main Hall

Opposite: William de Morgan, *Daisy* tile, c.1890s, first floor bedroom

In 1945 Baillie Scott moved to a Brighton nursing home where he died on the 10th February, aged 79. He was survived by a son, also named Mackay Hugh Baillie Scott, and a daughter, Enid Maud Mackay Hugh Baillie Scott. The epitaph carved on Baillie Scott's tombstone in Edenbridge Churchyard in Kent reads: *"Nature he loved, and Next to Nature, Art".*

Selected works by Mackay Hugh Baillie Scott:

1892-93   The Red House, Victoria Road, Douglas, Isle of Man

1897-98   Dining and drawing rooms (destroyed) Ducal Palace, Darmstadt, Germany

1897-98   Village Hall, Onchan, Isle of Man

1898-99   Blackwell, Windermere, (Westmorland), Cumbria

1899-1901 Police Station, Castle Rushen, Castletown, Isle of Man

1904-05 (c.) Elmwood Cottages, Letchworth, Herts

1907-11   Waldbühl, Uzwil, Switzerland

1908-09   Waterlow Court, Heath Close, Hampstead Garden Suburb

1912-13   House, 48 Storey's Way, Cambridge

1924   Church, Rate Corner, Maltings Lane, Cambridge

1928-9   Ashwood, Ashwood Road, Woking, Surrey

"Blackwell is the most important surviving example of Baillie Scott's work in England."

Martin Gayford, *Daily Telegraph*, January 1999

House & Garden

Blackwell's siting and orientation were key factors in its design; the house is perched on the hillside rather than down by the lake where already, by the 1890s, it was becoming almost suburban. The Lake District setting is further reinforced by the decoration inside, which takes rowan berries of the mountain ash as the principal motif in the downstairs rooms. Throughout the house wild flowers, berries and birds are found in the carvings, tiles, stained glass, plaster work and fabric frieze - all helping to reflect the natural environment outside.

Blackwell has a striking and impressive presence in the landscape. It is a grand statement, but Baillie Scott drew on elements of local vernacular architecture and reinterpreted them to his own purposes. Roughcast white-washed walls, steep pitched Westmorland slate roofs, cylindrical chimneys and multiple gables evoke Lakeland farmhouse architecture of the sixteenth and seventeenth centuries. Yet Baillie Scott's adaptation also produced an effect which is strikingly modern. Crisp sharp lines and minimal ornamentation create a complex orchestration of flat planes with sandstone window mullions set flush within the façades.

The house is beautifully integrated into the landscape, standing tall on the hillside with the White Drawing Room raised high, facing west and commanding wonderful views of Windermere and the Coniston fells beyond. Decorative elements are introduced on the outside of the building in the lead rainwater hoppers, some of which resemble castle turrets whilst others bear the initials of Edward Holt and the date, 1900, when Blackwell was completed. Holt's initials can also be seen in the original gates that have been re-hung on fine slate piers topped with sandstone spheres. These mark the original, but now privately owned, driveway up to Blackwell.

Baillie Scott saw the gardens and terraces as yet another series of rooms flowing out from the main house, and they were critical in defining the setting of Blackwell on its fellside site. We know from records that Thomas Mawson (1861-1933), the Windermere-based landscape designer, was involved in the design of the gardens. However, Baillie Scott may also have had some input as he had already worked on a number of garden designs. His most successful garden design was for Snowshill Manor in the

Above: Rainwater hopper
© Paul Barker / Country Life picture library 2005
Opposite: Blackwell from the Lower Terrace

Cotswolds in 1920, which is now owned by the National Trust and open to the public.

As this was only ever intended to be a holiday home, the gardens at Blackwell were quite simple and low maintenance, and, on the lower terrace, there were two lawn tennis courts. The series of terraces, arranged at different levels, are defined by substantial slate walls with giant buttresses. From each level the most important consideration was how to best experience the glorious views of the Lake District scenery.

The original plans for the gardens have not survived, although we can see the broad layout from early photographs. A new planting scheme has thus been implemented which is sympathetic to the architecture, whilst following the original principles of linking the house and garden with the surrounding landscape. The original planting scheme extended into the fields to the south of the house where several groups of trees and a small copse with rhododendrons were planted. This treatment creates the feeling that the whole of the Lake District is the garden, rather than a separate, defined area.

The modern planting scheme includes clematis, purple, red, pink and yellow tulips, crocusima 'Citronella', dahlia 'David Howard', 'Johnson's Blue' geranium, 'Berkley Gold' iris, marigolds, alliums, cornflowers and fragrant herbs including lavender, sage and fennel. Rowan trees have also been planted as they provided the inspiration for much of the interior decoration.

Above: Azalias
Below: Delphiniums
Opposite: Blackwell overlooking Windermere, 2008
© Tony West Photography 2009

The Principal Rooms

Throughout Blackwell Baillie Scott used every element an architect had at his disposal to the full. The house is a grand orchestration of light, space, colour, different materials and decorative detailing, creating a very special architectural experience.

The glowing interiors are a symphony of exuberant plasterwork, intricate metalwork, stained glass, stone work, William de Morgan tiles and carved panelling in honey coloured oak. In almost every room different designs of daisies, bluebells, roses, rowan, hawthorn and oak are depicted. Little birds can also be seen weaving in and out of the carved wooden screens and capitals or fluttering their wings in the stained glass. Despite the richness of decorative detail, however, the effect is not fussy or cluttered. Each element is incorporated skilfully into the overall scheme to give a marvellously integrated and cohesive whole.

Baillie Scott was very skilful in his use of light inside the house and orientated Blackwell with the main rooms facing south, rather than west across the lake, so that the maximum benefit can be gained from sunlight throughout the day.

Above: Delft tiles, the Main Hall fireplace
Opposite: The Main Hall © Nick Wood

The Main Hall

Baillie Scott was interested in challenging the tight planning of the typical Victorian house design to achieve a new open-plan spaciousness, and inside Blackwell the internal plan revolves around a large double-height hall. On entering the half-timbered Main Hall, one is taken back to medieval times. High above the oak panelling the eye is drawn to six stained glass windows, depicting Edward Holt's coat of arms (showing two fleur-de-lys between two stylised mountain ash trees) and those bodies with whom the Holts were associated; Rugby School, Exeter and Christ Church Colleges, Oxford, Manchester City and Manchester University.

"Blackwell is one of the most impressive and inspirational houses built in Britain... and stands at the crossroads of Victorian and modern architecture."

Anthony Skinner, *Lancashire Life*, August 2001

Above: M. H. Baillie Scott, Chair, oak, c.1895
Opposite: The Main Hall at the beginning of the 20th century, showing the billiard table. Notice the absence of the Peacock Frieze which was added in about 1905

As with a medieval hall, Blackwell's Main Hall would have been the principal entertaining area and a place for guests to gather and relax, and the space is made more fluid with the use of sliding doors. It also has a door opening onto the south lawn, allowing both physical and visual access to the gardens and also to the wider landscape beyond.

Playing billiards was a popular pursuit and Baillie Scott produced his own design for the six unusual dish-shaped beaten copper electric light shades that originally lit the billiard table. The photograph opposite shows the billiard table and how the lights would have been hung. They have been re-hung after being discovered, covered in years of dust, in a cupboard under the stairs soon after the Lakeland Arts Trust bought the house. It was odd, at this time, to give a billiard table such prominence; they were more commonly placed away from the central living area; however, this was a holiday home and would have been used somewhat differently to the main family house.

Intimate areas were created in the inglenook, with settles set either side of a generous fireplace of huge interlocking blocks of local Ancaster stone and Broughton slate, and a lining of delft tiles. These elements are reflected in the fireplace in the Dining Room, which is visible through the door opposite. A scaled down corner version of this fireplace design has survived upstairs in what would have been the only en-suite bathroom. The blue and white delft tiles are contemporary with Blackwell, despite the seventeenth century decorative motifs which further reinforce the baronial feel of the space.

Baillie Scott was in tune with the philosophy of John Ruskin, and throughout the house he incorporated Ruskin's belief that "Good art flows from the craftsmen who create it". Furthermore, Baillie Scott was a designer who preferred to work with local craftspeople, and he positively encouraged them to draw out the qualities of their materials. The lower parts of the walls are clad in oak wainscot, with an intricate frieze of intertwined rowan berries, carved by Simpsons of Kendal.

Baillie Scott's furnishing designs were intended to complement his architecture and followed the same principles of fine craftsmanship with simple and elegant forms, offering an alternative to the overcrowded and fussy interiors that dominated the later nineteenth

Above: M.H. Baillie Scott, Manxman Piano, c.1900
© Lakeland Arts Trust / Stuart Parker 2005

Below: Combination table and wall bracket lamp, c.1900
Designed by W.A.S. Benson, manufactured by W.A.S. Benson & Co. Ltd;
shade by James Powell & Sons, Whitefriars.
© Lakeland Arts Trust 2009

Opposite: Shand Kydd (designed by W. Dennington), *Peacock Frieze*
(detail), wallpaper, c.1900, the Main Hall

century. At Blackwell he also built in window or alcove seats in every room, which reduced the need for other furniture, allowing uninterrupted floor spaces.

One of the interesting pieces of furniture in the Main Hall is the 'Manxman' piano of around 1900, complete with a Broadwood movement, which was acquired for Blackwell by the Lakeland Arts Trust in 1999. Baillie Scott's design was cleverly disguised as an elegant, yet robust, cupboard with the keys hidden away behind doors decorated with horizontal strap-hinges. These hinges extend round the sides and end in a fleur-de-lys motif. When the doors are opened and the lid lifted, they act as sounding boards and serve to amplify the volume.

The piano was intended to look good in any room, not just in a music room, and it sits perfectly in the oak panelled Main Hall. The Holt family were all musically trained and an early photograph (illustrated on p.8) shows a piano in the same position. Visitors today are encouraged to play the piano, and sheet music from the period when Blackwell was built is provided.

The Peacock Frieze

The frieze in the Hall, which came from the popular Macclesfield wallpaper manufacturers Shand Kydd, has undergone careful conservation, which took nine months to complete. Hermann Muthesius, an architect attached to the German Embassy in London between 1896 and 1903, included Blackwell in his influential 1905 book *Das Englische Haus* (*The English House*), which examined domestic architecture at the beginning of the twentieth century. The 1905 photograph of the Hall in *Das Englische Haus* (illustrated on p. 24) shows the frieze to be absent, suggesting that it was a slightly later addition.

The Minstrel's Gallery

This small room sits above the main fireplace, which in turn creates the cosy inglenook beneath. It provides an elevated space within the Main Hall, perched like a small tree house. From this viewpoint

"It is at the fireside that the interest of the room is focused, and in our inconstant climate we may be driven, at almost any season of the year, to seek there that brightness and warmth which we fail to find in the outside world."

M. H. Baillie Scott, *The Studio*, 15 November 1895

Above: Block printed and stencilled hessian wall covering, the Dining Room (detail), designed by Baillie Scott
Opposite: The Dining Room fireplace

you can appreciate the true dimensions of the double-height hall. Earlier, in 1898, Baillie Scott had decorated and furnished a fantasy tree house, *'Le Nid'*, for the twenty-three-year-old Princess Marie of Romania, which did not survive.

His passion for all aspects of design, and his desire to create a unified whole, led Baillie Scott to design furniture and fabrics, such as the hessian wall covering in the Dining Room. He often gave his designs to craftspeople so that they could produce furniture and furnishings, and these were sold to the public through outlets such as Heal's and Liberty and Co.

The Dining Room

Like the Main Hall, the Dining Room incorporates some strikingly modern elements for the period. The treatment of the fireplace is skilfully handled and the stained glass on either side of it is strongly 'Art Nouveau' in its flowing organic lines.

Here, simple timber panelling acts as a foil to the main element of the room, the spectacular and extremely rare block-printed hessian wall covering. This has been painstakingly conserved, although the original blue background faded to brown a long time ago. Birds, daisies and bluebells are represented in the bold design, as well as the decorative theme of rowan berries found throughout the house.

Traditionally, family and guests would gather in the Drawing Room before being summoned for dinner by the butler. From here they would proceed through the hall to the dining room, which was darker and more sombre in character, warmed by a large fire. Dinner was taken at seven, and would always require formal dress. The butler, assisted by a maid, would serve several courses, and dinner would often last well into the evening. After dinner the ladies withdrew to the White Drawing Room for coffee, usually leaving the men to cigars, port and, perhaps, a game of billiards later.

"...we seem already to have stepped into the world of fantasy and romance of the ancient bardic poetry that was once supposed to have been the legacy of the misty figure of Ossian... With Baillie Scott we are among the purely Northern poets among British architects."

Hermann Muthesius (1867 - 1927)

Above: Stained glass window in the White Drawing Room
Opposite: The White Drawing Room

The White Drawing Room at Blackwell is considered to be one of Baillie Scott's finest interiors. In stark contrast to the masculine feel of the Main Hall, this room is delightfully romantic and feminine. Here, again, are carvings of birds, leaves, roses, hawthorn berries and acorns. These natural forms create an almost Byzantine richness in the ceiling plasterwork, which survives miraculously intact. Every part of the space has been considered to make the most of the Lakeland views and, in the early evening, golden sunlight floods into this room as the sun sets behind the Coniston fells.

The inglenook fireplace is the most complex and elegant in the house. It incorporates many different elements: stained glass, ceramic tiles, carved wooden capitals, alcoves, stonework, mosaic floor, a pair of wonderful iron and enamelled fire dogs and a double mantel. The mantel shelf is not confined only to the fireplace, but metamorphoses into a shelf that could be used for the display of ceramics, which extends around the room, supported on slender columns. These tapering poles are topped with capitals of carved wood that branch out to reveal little birds, fruits and leaves. More birds dart between swaying tulips illuminated in the stained glass. Small mirrors set into the panelling give further brilliance to the light flooding in from the landscape that dances around the room throughout the day.

Finally, there is a beautifully restrained bay window affording magnificent views across the lake to the Coniston fells. Light not only falls from the sky, but is also reflected upwards from the lake onto the ceiling, bringing into sharp relief the intricate plasterwork. This window also falls along the axis of the main corridor and serves to create the dramatic crescendo of light which draws you along its length.

Above: M. H. Baillie Scott, Fire dog (detail), wrought iron and enamel, c.1900 © Nick Wood 2005
Below: 'Sussex' armchair, ebonised beech and rush. Designed by D.G. Rossetti, manufactured by Morris, Marshall, Faulkner & Company, c.1880
Opposite: The White Drawing Room

Colour

Colour plays a vital role in the interior decoration at Blackwell. Downstairs this is achieved largely by the combination of different materials, such as the warm rich tones of honey coloured oak panelling, green slate set against pink sandstone, copper light fittings, and different coloured marbles to create vibrant mosaics. Baillie Scott researched in some depth the effect of colour on people's moods, and he often chose blue in the dining room for its calming qualities.

The upper floors once provided generous accommodation for the Holts and their five children, as well as for house guests. Paint analysis revealed the colour schemes of the different rooms to be very bold - ranging from strong green to bright yellow. The colours of the walls related to those in the beautiful William de Morgan tiles gracing the fireplaces, as well as to those found in the stained glass windows.

The architect Roderick Gradidge writes about Blackwell in his book 'Dream Houses: The Edwardian Ideal' –

"For Baillie Scott there were three basic colour schemes. The first one was the dark colours that he used in dining rooms . . . The two other schemes relied on a great deal of white, most of Baillie Scott's furniture design being enamelled white or lightly stained an 'artistic' green. His pure white interiors often rely on a very sharp contrast of golden orange, perhaps combined with a pale blue or light purple and pink. It was these elegant, rather feminine colours that he considered suitable for drawing rooms. In bedrooms on the other hand he tended to use khaki greens, once again set off with intense patches of purple and pink. The palette is always very light and very clean, the watercolour washes seem almost to come straight from the tube without any mixing, and the contrast with the rather heavy colours of even such artistic designers of an earlier generation as William Morris and Norman Shaw is enormous."

"…at Blackwell with its friezes of sapphire and emerald-coloured peacocks, and windows glittering with coloured glass of bluebirds and tulips, there is a real resonance between the Art Nouveau objects and the interiors of the house."

Sue Herdman, *BBC Homes and Antiques*, August 2004

The Arts & Crafts Bedroom

There is no photographic evidence of how the Holts would have furnished the upstairs rooms, however it is clear from paint analysis that this room would have been painted a golden yellow, as it is today. The Bedroom and Dressing Room enjoy spectacular views of the lake and have largely been furnished with furniture and objects on loan to the Lakeland Arts Trust. These include a mirror designed by Eric Gill and carved with poetry by Robert Burns, and an example of a brass wall light designed by Baillie Scott. The impressive pendant ceiling lights (c.1900) were specially sourced for the house and made by the large manufacturer G.E.C.

Corridors

The corridors are key architectural elements linking the principal rooms, both visually and in terms of access. In the ground floor corridor there are windows into the Main Hall as well as to the outside, the space flows from one area to another. The sliding doors are another clever device that totally alters the spatial relationships, depending on whether they are open or closed. Outside the White Drawing Room the passage widens, its panelling painted white, and carved columns are introduced in anticipation of the brilliant white room you are about to enter.

The upstairs landing is equally complex, with different levels of light provided by both external and internal windows and skylights. The levels change as you move along the landing and, at three different points, the corridor expands to break the rhythm and create deep bays, which almost become separate rooms in their own right.

Above: William de Morgan, *Daisy* tile, c.1890s, an upstairs fireplace
Below: The upstairs corridor from the landing
Opposite: The Arts & Crafts Bedroom showing the Baillie Scott wall light

Edwardian Life

Blackwell was designed as a holiday home, a place of relaxation, a place to get away from the stresses of city life. The traditional and seasonal country pursuits of the aristocracy: hunting, shooting and the management of great estates, gave way to new pastimes, as the upper middle classes moved into their weekend retreats, or returned to the new garden suburbs. Arts & Crafts architects like Baillie Scott specialised in providing country houses for this growing and increasingly prosperous class.

Newly wealthy families, like the Holts, had no ancestral country seat so they commissioned architects to provide them with a house that would include elements of both country manor house and suburban villa. Tennis, rowing, sailing, music and billiards were the pastimes that Baillie Scott accommodated in his design.

Most importantly, the subtle planning of the house and gardens encouraged the Holts to lead a less formal life, opening out the living space and removing some of the rigid definitions common to nineteenth century interiors. The hall, far from being designed as an entrance space, took its inspiration from the medieval living hall, the hub of the home. It was a multi-purpose room, complete with billiard table, which anticipated the "open plan" scheme popular today. Nothing could be further from the social conventions of the day than Baillie Scott's assertion that halls were a good place for children's play!

Blackwell was the perfect place for entertaining guests. A suite of guest rooms was included in the east wing of the house, and the hall's great expanse of floor could accommodate a large gathering. The simple floor plan skilfully accommodated many of the elements demanded for correct social etiquette, with hall, dining room and drawing room fulfilling different roles. At Blackwell, like many other houses of the period, there is a clear definition between the rooms traditionally associated with masculine and feminine pursuits.

The drawing room was primarily for the ladies of the house, for receiving female guests and discussions over afternoon tea. Often, on these occasions, the hostess made tea herself, serving guests from a spirit kettle. Evening gatherings where both sexes could meet informally were also held in the drawing room, with piano playing, singing and playing cards. Baillie Scott cleverly provided built-in seating for a relatively large gathering, as well as more intimate areas for private conversation.

Above: Sailing boats on Windermere, c.1895
Below: Steamboat *Esperance*
Opposite: Joseph Holt pictured with the family dogs standing by the sundial, designed by Baillie Scott, which can still be seen today on the South Terrace, c.1905

Above: Wrought iron window latch (detail)
© Lakeland Arts Trust / Charlotte Wood 2005
Opposite: Blackwell, summer 2008
© Tony West Photography, 2009

The Servant Question

Blackwell was designed to accommodate a large number of servants, necessary for carrying out most household tasks mainly without the help of mechanical aids. As well as having live-in staff, a number of servants would also be sent to Blackwell, in advance of a visit, to prepare the house. Nearly half of the floor space is dedicated to domestic staff and services, which helps to explain its 'L' shape plan incorporating a service wing. Baillie Scott was concerned that servants were given rooms that were pleasant and well lit, and at Blackwell there was comparatively little difference between servants' and guest accommodation. The servants' rooms, in the second floor attics, are now the archive, library and offices. Some permanent staff lived in the two lodges, which are now in private ownership.

The servants' hall and kitchens were placed at the front of the house so that staff could observe the entrance and the two driveways. Additionally, it was customary to locate the Butler's and Housekeeper's pantries between the service wing and the family areas of the house. As senior members of the staff they ran the household from these rooms, often dining separately from the rest of the servants. One of these rooms is now the shop and reception, and the other is now part of the new staircase and lift. These spaces had previously been adapted for school and office use and, as a result, few original features had survived.

By 1900 it was becoming obvious that the diminishing numbers of available staff would cause problems for households like the Holts'. What was known at the time as the "servant question" meant that houses like Blackwell were becoming difficult to run. After the Second World War houses were designed that relied less on servants and more on modern technology, and there was no longer the need to provide so much accommodation for live-in staff.

Recent History & Restoration

After their eldest son died in the First World War, the Holts used Blackwell less and less. From this time on, Blackwell remained more or less empty apart from a skeleton staff of servants keeping an eye on the place. Occasional visits were still made, but the family seemed to have somewhat lost interest in Blackwell. This lack of interest, however, is what has enabled Blackwell to survive so remarkably intact. Subsequent occupants of the building never actually owned it, and thus were not in a position to make significant alterations. The Holts, who by this time were leasing the house, also had little incentive to use their money on modernising a property that was of little personal interest to them. As a consequence of this series of historical circumstances, most of the original features of Blackwell were thankfully still in place when it came to the notice of the Lakeland Arts Trust.

Blackwell had been given a new lease of life during the Second World War, when pupils from Huyton College in Liverpool were evacuated there. One room has displays telling the history of Blackwell, and is named 'Miss Murphy's Room' in memory of a very special former Headmistress. After the war Blackwell continued as a school, finally closing in 1976. One of the garden terraces has been named in memory of the late Miss Jean McGowan, who taught at Blackwell for many years, and her companion, the late Miss Kay Dobie, who also worked at the school. Strong supporters of the Blackwell restoration project from the very beginning, they provided fascinating information about the history of the school as well as helping re-unite former pupils.

When the school closed, Blackwell was bought by a Yorkshire businessman, Maurice Bland, who leased it as offices to the English Conservancy Council, later renamed English Nature. During their occupancy the scope of the decorative detail inside Blackwell was hidden from view behind boarded-up fireplaces and rows of filing cabinets. As a result, the delicate fittings were somewhat protected from modern office use.

In 1997 English Nature moved out and the future of Blackwell was suddenly uncertain. Fearing that this treasure trove of the Arts & Crafts, which at that time only carried the lowest grade listing, could be irreparably damaged, the Lakeland Arts Trust stepped in.

Above: Blackwell, c.1940
Below: Girls skating at Blackwell in the 1940s when it was a school
Opposite: Double vaulted bedroom undergoing restoration in 2000
© Lakeland Arts Trust 2009

An approach to the owner to buy the house was quickly made even though, at that point, the building was not actually for sale and there were no funds for the purchase!

It was then a race against time to raise the money, first for the purchase, and then for the restoration of Blackwell. It was an enormous task and involved many difficult negotiations and a tremendous amount of hard work, which was given freely by many of the people working on the project. Bit by bit the pieces fell into place. Within ten months of starting the fund-raising campaign, a combination of money raised, together with interest free loans from two generous individuals, enabled the Trust to buy Blackwell in February 1999. Over the next year or two we received fantastic support from many private donors, as well as charitable trusts and foundations. Finally, the Trust was given a grant of £2.252 million from the Heritage Lottery Fund, which allowed us to proceed with Blackwell's full restoration.

This took just over a year and involved a great number of specialists in many different fields, including Allies and Morrison, the project architects, and English Heritage, who raised Blackwell's listing status to the highest level of Grade I. His Royal Highness The Prince of Wales supported the project from early on, visiting the house just before the restoration started, and, in September 2001, he visited Blackwell again to officially open the house to the public.

Above: Repairing the roof in 2000
© Lakeland Arts Trust 2009

Below: Restoring the Peacock Frieze 2000
© Lakeland Arts Trust 2009

Opposite above: Blackwell under wraps!
© Lakeland Arts Trust 2009

Opposite below: Cleaning the panelling in the Main Hall.
The white band above shows where the Peacock Frieze had been removed for conservation in 2000.
© Lakeland Arts Trust 2009

The Lakeland Arts Trust

Above: Abbot Hall Art Gallery in Kendal, summer 2008.
© Tony West Photography
Opposite: Francis Dodd, *Self Portrait*, etching, 1914

The Lakeland Arts Trust aims to bring enjoyment and inspiration to people's lives through art and history. It is a relatively small independent charity (No.526980), with an enthusiastic and dedicated team of staff. The Trust administers Abbot Hall Art Gallery in Kendal as well as Blackwell. Both houses are Grade I listed buildings, and each was saved, restored by the Trust, and opened to the public.

Each building has its own characteristics, but both provide very special settings in which to see and enjoy art. Large national and local authority art galleries have a valuable role to play, but Abbot Hall and Blackwell allow a completely different experience, which is much more intimate and personal. Increasingly people (and particularly artists) are coming to realise how the particular circumstances of where art is placed can have a profound effect on the experience we get from it. Whether a Henry Moore sculpture is sited in a windswept moorland landscape, or a painting is seen in the serene vaulting of a cathedral, the effect can often be much more powerful and telling. Abbot Hall provides this alternative approach for painting and sculpture, whilst the exhibitions at Blackwell focus on craft and the applied arts. There is a strong emphasis on education, aimed at people of all ages and from all walks of life. Special attention is directed at young people, in the hope of lighting that spark of interest that is so often necessary to start a lifelong journey of discovering the inspiration that art can bring.

Abbot Hall Art Gallery has a high reputation for both its permanent collection and its changing exhibition programme. With no obligations to show particular types of art, nor to any other organisation, the gallery is able to select worthwhile exhibitions and artists that have a significant contribution to make to the arts. Recent important exhibitions have included work by Walter Richard Sickert, Stanley Spencer, Euan Uglow, Lucian Freud, Bridget Riley, Paula Rego, Sean Scully, David Bomberg, Ruskins and Turners from Tate, and watercolours from the Royal Collection. Items from the Abbot Hall collection of applied arts and twentieth century fine art and craft, that were previously hidden from view in storage, are now on display at Blackwell, where they can be seen and enjoyed.

In the Spring of 2007 the Trust entered an exciting new phase of development when it took charge of the nearby Windermere Steamboat Museum, embarking on a major project to restore its world class collection of vintage steamboats. Many of the boats in the collection were built as pleasure craft for the likes of Sir Edward Holt at the turn of the last century. A grant from the National Heritage Memorial Fund has funded the first phase of the project and more money will be needed in the coming years to restore all the boats and to create an exciting new building complex on this stunning lakeshore site.

Study and Research

The Margaret Lawler Study Room includes many books on architecture, garden design, and the Arts & Crafts, as well as numerous other related books and periodicals. On long term loan from the Art Workers' Guild, there is the Roderick Gradidge collection; a library of specialist books that belonged to the architect and architectural historian, who died in 2000. Funds from the Aurelius Trust are helping us to purchase more books and periodicals for the collection.

The library is available, by appointment, for research purposes by those visiting Blackwell, and it is a wonderful resource.

Above: S. L. Osprey, 1902
Below: Books with cover designs by Talwin Morris
Opposite: Christopher Dresser, *Claret Jug*, glass, silver and ebony, c.1881. On loan from the Art Workers' Guild

Friends, Patrons & Benefactors

As well as supporting study and research, the Trust has ongoing expenses in maintaining Blackwell and we also wish to purchase more objects and furniture for the house. If you would like to support the work we do, you can become a Friend, Patron or Benefactor of the Lakeland Arts Trust. Details can be obtained from Blackwell, by post, telephone, email or from the website: **www.lakelandartstrust.org.uk**

Acknowledgements

The Blackwell restoration would not have been possible without the generous donations of many individuals, some of whom wish to remain anonymous. A number of rooms and areas have been named and are listed below:

The Herbaceous Terrace in memory of Miss Jean McGowan and Miss Kay Dobie.

The Oliver Thompson Room.

Restoration of the Peacock Frieze and Hall funded by the Naylor family.

The Muncaster Terrace in memory of Phill Jacobs.

Restoration of the Dining Room funded by the Pilgrim Trust.

The Jocelyn Morton Room.

The Library in memory of Margaret Lawler.

Restoration of the Minstrel's Gallery in memory of Isaac Rhodes.

The Archive Room in memory of Mabel and Elsie Longmire.

The ground floor passageway oak panelling restored in memory of Marian Cowgill.

The wrought iron work restoration funded by Dr Philip Welch.

We would like to thank the following for their assistance with the research of this guide: John Borron, Dr Jenni Brunton, Joan Bangor Jones and Huyton College Old Girls, Richard Kershaw, Simon Elliot, Diane Haigh, Peter Kelly, Gillian Riding, Simon Smith, Gavin Stamp, Tim Sturgis, Professor David Walker and Cherrie Trelogan.

Above: C. F. A. Voysey, Trivet, brass and iron, c.1909

Blackwell

The Arts & Crafts House

Bowness-on-Windermere
Cumbria
LA23 3JT
United Kingdom
T 015394 46139
F 015394 88486
E info@blackwell.org.uk
www.blackwell.org.uk

LAKELANDARTSTRUST

ISBN No. 1-902498-29-1